PUBLIC LIBRARY, DISTRICT OF COLUMBIA

D1217837

SUPER CUTE!

Baby Giraffes

by Megan Borgert-Spaniol

BLASTOFF! READERS

BELLWETHER MEDIA · MINNEAPOLIS, MN

Note to Librarians, Teachers, and Parents:

Blastoff! Readers are carefully developed by literacy experts and combine standards-based content with developmentally appropriate text.

Level 1 provides the most support through repetition of high-frequency words, light text, predictable sentence patterns, and strong visual support.

Level 2 offers early readers a bit more challenge through varied simple sentences, increased text load, and less repetition of high-frequency words.

Level 3 advances early-fluent readers toward fluency through increased text and concept load, less reliance on visuals, longer sentences, and more literary language.

Level 4 builds reading stamina by providing more text per page, increased use of punctuation, greater variation in sentence patterns, and increasingly challenging vocabulary.

Level 5 encourages children to move from "learning to read" to "reading to learn" by providing even more text, varied writing styles, and less familiar topics.

Whichever book is right for your reader, Blastoff! Readers are the perfect books to build confidence and encourage a love of reading that will last a lifetime!

This edition first published in 2016 by Bellwether Media, Inc.

No part of this publication may be reproduced in whole or in part without written permission of the publisher. For information regarding permission, write to Bellwether Media, Inc., Attention: Permissions Department, 5357 Penn Avenue South, Minneapolis, MN 55419.

Library of Congress Cataloging-in-Publication Data

Borgert-Spaniol, Megan, 1989- author.
  Baby Giraffes / by Megan Borgert-Spaniol.
    pages cm. – (Blastoff! Readers. Super Cute!)
  Summary: "Developed by literacy experts for students in kindergarten through grade three, this book introduces baby giraffes to young readers through leveled text and related photos"– Provided by publisher.
  Audience: Ages 5-8
  Audience: K to grade 3
  Includes bibliographical references and index.
  ISBN 978-1-62617-216-6 (hardcover: alk. paper)
  1. Giraffe–Infancy–Juvenile literature. I. Title. II. Series: Blastoff! Readers. 1, Super Cute!
  QL737.U56B67 2016
  599.638–dc23
                          2015009729

Text copyright © 2016 by Bellwether Media, Inc. BLASTOFF! READERS and associated logos are trademarks and/or registered trademarks of Bellwether Media, Inc. SCHOLASTIC, CHILDREN'S PRESS, and associated logos are trademarks and/or registered trademarks of Scholastic Inc.

Printed in the United States of America, North Mankato, MN.

Table of Contents

Giraffe Calf!

A baby giraffe is called a calf. It is 6 feet (1.8 meters) tall when born.

Time With Mom

The calf drops to the ground during birth. Mom licks her **newborn** clean.

The calf stands within an hour. Now it can drink mom's milk.

Mom **nuzzles** her calf to show love. This is how they **bond**.

Staying Safe

The calf hides between mom's legs. Mom will kick **predators** that come close.

Sometimes mom leaves to go eat. The calf hides in tall grass or bushes.

The baby's **coat** has spots. These marks help it to blend in.

Joining the Herd

Soon it is time to join the **herd**. The herd is made up of females and their babies.

Now the calf can play with other young giraffes. New friends!

Glossary

bond—to become close

coat—the hair or fur covering an animal

herd—a group of giraffes that travel together

newborn—a baby that was just recently born

nuzzles—softly rubs up against with the nose or forehead

predators—animals that hunt other animals for food

To Learn More

AT THE LIBRARY

Andreae, Giles. *Giraffes Can't Dance*. New York, N.Y.: Cartwheel Books, 2012.

Doudna, Kelly. *It's a Baby Giraffe!* Edina, Minn.: ABDO Publishing Company, 2009.

Schuetz, Kari. *Giraffes*. Minneapolis, Minn.: Bellwether Media, 2012.

ON THE WEB

Learning more about giraffes is as easy as 1, 2, 3.

1. Go to www.factsurfer.com.

2. Enter "giraffes" into the search box.

3. Click the "Surf" button and you will see a list of related web sites.

With factsurfer.com, finding more information is just a click away.

Index

The images in this book are reproduced through the courtesy of: Photoshot/ Newscom, front cover; Villiers Steyn, pp. 4-5; Sebastian/ Alamy, pp. 6-7; Erwin Niemand, pp. 6-7 (bottom); Europics/ Newscom, pp. 8-9; Andrzej Kubik, pp. 8-9 (bottom); James D. Morgan/ REX/ Newscom, pp. 10-11; Minden Pictures/ Superstock, pp. 12-13; Dmussman, pp. 12-13 (bottom); Dr Ajay Kumar Singh, pp. 14-15; Hoffman Photography/ Age Fotostock, pp. 16-17; Konrad Wothe/ Glow Images, pp. 18-19; Holger Holleman/ Corbis, pp. 20-21.

FEB 0 8 2016